Perspectives
Watching Every Move You Make
You Make
Privacy vs. Security

Flying Start
to Literacy®

Contents

Introduction

What is the balance between privacy and security?

Privacy is important. So how do you feel about being watched when you're at the shops, your car being tracked or your phone conversations being listened to? We are under constant surveillance by high-tech cameras and satellites, and it's done to keep us safe. Cameras help catch criminals, tracking devices help find people and satellites can track storms.

A question that concerns many people in our society is: Are we going too far?

SYSTEM
RECOGNITION
IN PROGRESS ...

56%

BIOMETRIC IDENTIFICATION : ON - OBJECTS DETECTION : ON - BEHAVIOR ANALYSIS :

5

Why spy?

Are you being spied on? In this article, Michael Hedges argues that in today's world, much of what we do and say is no longer private. More and more of what we do is monitored in an attempt to keep everybody safe.

But Michael presents some very convincing reasons for the need for surveillance technology. See if he convinces you!

Think about what you did today. Perhaps you went to school or the shops. Did you ever think that you were being watched? In many cases, somebody – or *something* – was watching you and recording details of your everyday life.

The technology used for surveillance keeps getting better and better, so many of the things you do each day are recorded by closed-circuit television (CCTV). Is this fair? Is this right? You may not think it is, but there are usually good reasons for most of the surveillance that is done.

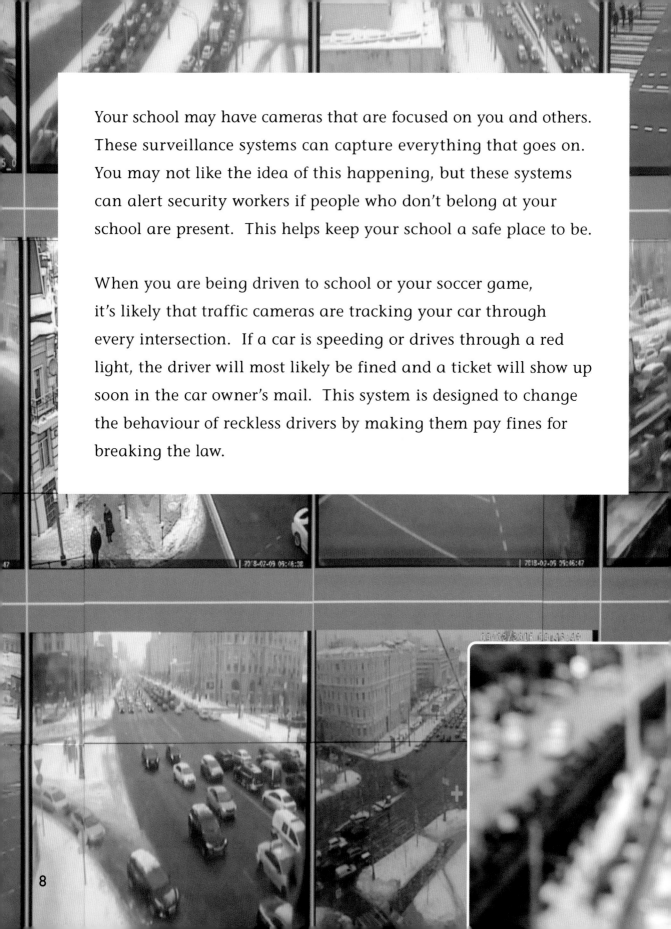

Your school may have cameras that are focused on you and others. These surveillance systems can capture everything that goes on. You may not like the idea of this happening, but these systems can alert security workers if people who don't belong at your school are present. This helps keep your school a safe place to be.

When you are being driven to school or your soccer game, it's likely that traffic cameras are tracking your car through every intersection. If a car is speeding or drives through a red light, the driver will most likely be fined and a ticket will show up soon in the car owner's mail. This system is designed to change the behaviour of reckless drivers by making them pay fines for breaking the law.

When you turn on your mobile phone, a tracking device inside it records your location so people know where you are. Sometimes, law enforcement agencies monitor phone calls and emails, and the information they gather by doing this can help them fight crime.

There are cameras along many city streets and in shops. The footage recorded by these cameras can be used by police to catch criminals.

In the future, you and other young people will have to work hard to strike the balance you want between privacy and security.

Keeping your data safe: Does it matter?

With over half the people in the world online daily, should we be worried about cyber safety?

Nic Gillespie tells us what he thinks about keeping his personal data safe. How does he try to convince you? Do you agree with Nic?

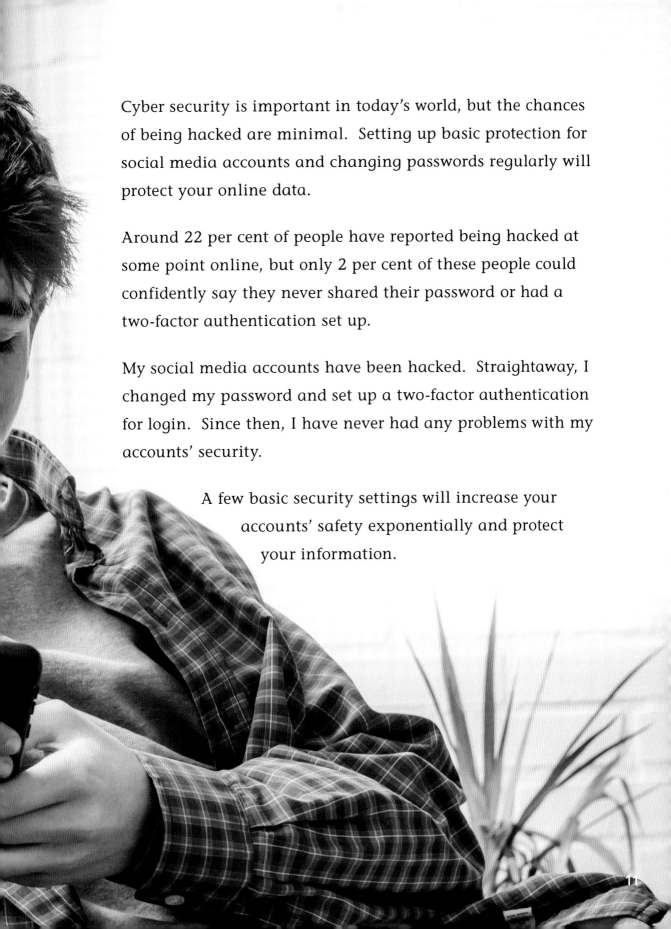

Cyber security is important in today's world, but the chances of being hacked are minimal. Setting up basic protection for social media accounts and changing passwords regularly will protect your online data.

Around 22 per cent of people have reported being hacked at some point online, but only 2 per cent of these people could confidently say they never shared their password or had a two-factor authentication set up.

My social media accounts have been hacked. Straightaway, I changed my password and set up a two-factor authentication for login. Since then, I have never had any problems with my accounts' security.

A few basic security settings will increase your accounts' safety exponentially and protect your information.

It is also said that 45 per cent of all social media accounts are hacked by people the owner of the account knows, and that the hackers are able to gain access because the owner has told them their password.

Out of my friends that have been hacked, in every instance it has been by someone they knew who thought it would be funny to log in to the account and post something as a joke.

While online, if you are an ordinary person, you don't have much to worry about because most hackers wouldn't waste their time hacking a kid's social media account for laughs. Most serious hackers would aim for celebrities, high-ranking business people and members of government – or anyone with a credit card!

Today, around 3.48 billion people in the world have a social media account. What are the chances of a hacker picking your social media account to hack? I would say the chances are low – one in 3.48 billion. That seems like pretty good odds to me!

When you are on the Internet, staying safe and protecting your privacy is important – but it is not worth stressing over.

Controlling social media

Ella Hastings was surprised when her best friend posted a hurtful message about her on social media.

How do you stay safe on social media? What do you think about Ella's decisions?

Social media used to be my favourite place to share photos and videos – and to connect and stay connected with friends. But I found out that it is also a place for bullying. Not everyone is who they say they are. People can easily pretend and you can easily be attacked. This is what happened to me.

I love drawing and to do this I need special pencils. The very best pencils are expensive. *Do I really need them?* I thought. *But one day, I will have a set of those pencils.* And guess what! For my birthday, my mum gave me a box of those beautiful pencils. I was so happy and so very excited. I took them to school and showed my friends.

Later in the day, I noticed that people were whispering and looking at me. Something was wrong! Then I looked on my phone. There I was with my new pencils, and there was a message from my friend Amy:

Amy 13:08 PM

Where did these pencils come from? Bella had a set just like that and now they have disappeared. Strange!

I couldn't believe it. Amy burst into tears when I showed her the message. "'That's not me," she said. "Someone must have hacked into my account!"

We told our teacher what had happened. I showed her my box of pencils. They were brand-new; the pencils had not been used. Bella was the only other person we knew who had pencils like these, but she had been using hers for a long time. I had not taken her pencils.

Our teacher talked to the class and told the whole story. Someone had done a very spiteful, hurtful thing, she said. Everyone listened, but I am sure there were still some people who didn't quite believe Amy or me.

I don't know if it was the right thing to do, but I shut down my account and since then, I've tried to distance myself from social media. But it was hard because social media is very addictive. When you don't use social media for a while, you can feel disconnected from your personal-friendship world and sometimes a bit left out.

What's the password?

How do you keep your personal information safe online?
Here, our expert, Constance Gibbs, shares her tips.

What password can you make? How strong is it?

Step 1

Choose a fun and memorable phrase, the longer the better:

Taylor Swift is my favourite singer

Step 2

Type the first two letters from each word:

TaSwismyfasi

Step 3

Replace some of the letters with numbers or symbols that look like the letters they replace:

Ta5wismyf@5l

A live map of Earth:

Creepy or cool?

Today, powerful satellites that orbit Earth can capture images of objects on the planet that are just 25 centimetres across. This gives new meaning to the phrase "someone to watch over me", writes Kathryn Hulick.

Read what Kathryn has to say on the privacy versus safety issue. What information did you find most persuasive? What is your opinion?

In 2014, a powerful new satellite was launched into space. It was the WorldView-3 satellite. Even though it orbits Earth at more than 600 kilometres away, it can make out a smartphone held in your hand. It can also tell what types of cars are travelling down a road, but it can't identify your face or read your car's number plate, or so they say.

But imagine turning on the GPS and seeing an image of your car from above. As the car drives, the map follows along in real time, alerting you to any traffic, pedestrians, animals or other things nearby. Routes and names of roads appear over the livestream. It's like the map has come to life.

This type of map isn't available yet. But it could be soon. According to some reports, this satellite and other spy satellites have the technology to take even sharper images.

Live, detailed maps of Earth's surface could aid humanity in amazing ways. Satellite images can help experts track storms as they form and then chart their paths.

At high detail, live maps of a disaster area could quickly reveal people in need of rescue, as well as the safest routes in or out.

Satellite images are already helping law enforcement officials catch illegal logging and fishing operations. Higher detail may make it possible to catch other criminals in the act. The images could also make it easier for farmers to watch over their crops or for prospectors to find minerals.

But many countries have laws that forbid making these super-sharp pictures public, to prevent enemies from using them. The idea that anybody might be able to spy on the entire earth in such detail seems creepy. What do you think?

What is your opinion? How to write a persuasive argument

1. State your opinion

Think about the issues related to your topic. What is your opinion?

2. Research

Research the information you need to support your opinion.

Related *Perspectives* book   Internet   Other sources

3. Make a plan

Introduction

How will you "hook" the reader?

State your opinion.

List reasons to support your opinion.

What persuasive devices will you use?

Reason 1	**Reason 2**	**Reason 3**
Support your reason with evidence and details.	Support your reason with evidence and details.	Support your reason with evidence and details.

Conclusion

Restate your opinion. Leave your reader with a strong message.

4. Publish

Publish your persuasive argument.

Use visuals to reinforce your opinion.